I THOUGHT I'D DANCE

I THOUGHT I'D DANCE

100 Books In 100 Days

Collection

#10

Pamela Denise Brown

Author

Publisher

Illustrator

Editor

ACKNOWLEDGEMENT

I Would Like To Acknowledge The CREATOR OF HEAVEN AND EARTH (GOD) FOR ALL THAT HE HAS Given Me. Thanking God I Am For My Talents and Gifts.

I Recognize That The Lord Gave Me This Gift, Which Allows Me To Share With Children And Everyone That Participates In The Reading Of The Literary Material That I Produce Through The Commission Of God.

Thank You Lord God

I Will Forever Be Grateful

For Your Trust In Me

Pamela Denise Brown

Pamelainthelight Publications/Books Speak For You books may be ordered through booksellers or by contacting:

Books Speak For You
A Division Of Pamelainthelight Publications
Philadelphia, PA
Booksspeakforyou.com
Pamelainthelight.com
267-454-3317

ISBN: 978-1-943611-37-9
Library of Congress Control Number:

Printed in the United States Of America

Books Speak For You (Non Profit Children's Division)
A Division Of Pamelainthelight Publications

DEDICATION

*I dedicate this book and EVERY BOOK I WRITE to my
Mother (Queen-Ella Brown) who NEVER STOPS
BELIEVING IN ME, WHO IS ALWAYS BY MY SIDE AND
HAS ALWAYS PARTICIPATED IN THE SUCCESS OF
WHO I AM AS A PERSON, THANK YOU MOM FOR
BEING WHO YOU ARE
To My children
Carrayah Queen-Ella,
Gabriel Joel
&
Carrynn Erin-Josette.
LOVING YOU ALL, I AM FOREVER
I also dedicate this book to all Children, Parents,
Guardians, Mothers, Fathers, Teachers, Principals,
Librarians, Pediatricians, Therapist, Counselors,
Thought Leaders and every person that has anything to
do with the positive and successful development of
children in the world.
Continue to be an inspiration and motivator to the
children that are entrusted to the cultivation of your
expertise.*

Thank You

I Remain,

Pamela Denise Brown

THE BOOKS

100 BOOKS IN 100 DAYS

I was commissioned by God to write 100 books in 100 days on October 1, 2015,

Completion Day January 8, 2016.

This is the **10**th Book Of the 100.

My Collection Of Books are designed to foster the social development of children. I believe the books I write will transform the minds of children. My Books are designed to effectuate change and influence success in the lives of children.

The Books in the Collection are Reinforcements to Learning. If understood and used in collaboration with the academic curriculum that children are given, the books will help build their self-esteem and confidence to a level that would help them socially engage in a diverse world with confidence and ultimately prepare them for life.

Pamela Denise Browns'

QUOTES

If You're In A "CROWDED" Room and

A Child Is Sitting "ALONE" that can
only mean the room is EMPTY.....
> 11/21/2105 1:42 a.m.

Children Stand silently trying to

open a door that cannot be opened with
hands......
> 11/23/2015 11:18 a.m.`

INTRODUCTION

I Thought I'd Dance is about a girl who tries to discover herself through dancing.......It IS A LOVELY read.

The rhythm of the read has an attractive likable catch that has you dancing with yourself.

In the imagination of the READ, dancing is ILLUMINATED in the mind of everyone reading it.

It is grand in its introduction and the journey evokes the MIND, whisking it to a place where the DANCE IS discovered in the discovery of dancing.

Every Book in the Collection is designed to effectuate change in the lives of children and influence success. In addition, the collection of books is tools to help children engage socially in a diverse world with confidence and ultimately prepare them for life. I believe the books in the Collection are also tools to psychologically rouse children to become positive, culturally sensitive, confident, unbiased and trustworthy. The books will also give children a sense of social consciousness to be socially aware.

Sitting In My Silent Room,
  Looking through my window.......

Looking at the sun light bloom.......
Looking through my window.......

Reaching up within my mind.......

Trying to find my way inside.......

Inside me.......

I THOUGHT I'D DANCE.......

I thought I'd dance to bring the rain.......

I thought I'd dance so I could reign.......

Standing in the doorway grey.......

My thoughts parade and then they fade.......

I THOUGHT I'D DANCE.......

I thought I'd dance to free myself.......

I thought I'd dance to be myself.......

I thought I'd dance, thinking I could be GREAT......

Doing what would gain the BREAK.......

I THOUGHT I'D DANCE.......

I thought I'd dance to prove to you that dancing would be good to do…….

I THOUGHT I'D DANCE…….

Putting all my thoughts aside, laying down the feel of PRIDE.......

I THOUGHT I'D DANCE.......

I thought I'd dance to embrace what's true.......
To follow a path that I once knew.......

Searching for that peace within, I find when I'm
Chiming in.......

In my soul I search to find.......
That special place within my mind......

I THOUGHT I'D DANCE.......

I thought I'd dance to measure up, to those who
LOOK UP
.....and STIR me UP.......

LIFT me UP.......BUILD me UP,
    CLOSE UP.......

I THOUGHT I'D DANCE.......

I thought I'd dance to ENCOURAGE you.......
     To SHOW you......
You could do it too.......

I THOUGHT I'D DANCE.......

Studying how to do it WELL.......
Shaping my mind.......DEFINED and DESIGNED.......

I THOUGHT I'D DANCE.......

I thought I'd dance to have a ball.......
   I thought I'd dance to enjoy the call.......

The call for me to dance the scene.......
  The play, the act, in film and screen.......

I THOUGHT I'D DANCE.......

Discovering what I could be.......

.......I SEARCH AND SEARCH to find in ME.......

A place that only I COULD SEE.......
Expressing dance abroad FREELY.......

I THOUGHT I'D DANCE.......

I thought I'd dance to see the SUN.......

I thought I'd dance to see the MOON......

I thought I'd dance to be my BEST.......

I thought I'd dance to past the TEST.......

I thought I'd dance to face MYSELF.......

I thought I'd dance to be MYSELF.......

I thought I'd dance to CONCENTRATE.......

I thought I'd dance to become GREAT.......

I thought I'd dance to show the WORLD......

I thought I'd dance to change the TIME.......

I thought I'd dance to keep the PEACE.......

TO DANCE.......
TO DANCE.......
To SET ME FREE......

I THOUGHT I'D DANCE.......

PEOPLE TO BE ACKNOWLEDGED WHO ACKNOWLEDGED ME
MY FIRST RUN.......

The Authors Show is a place where authors are given an opportunity to have their work acknowledged through web based radio and/or television interview. A place where you can be recognized for your literary accomplishments and sat on a platform where you're worked is viewed and appreciated. The Authors show was the first place I interviewed and for that I AM GRATEFUL... This is a thank you to the Authors Show and a **SPECIAL Thank You to Linda Thompson, who interviewed me......**

THANK YOU LINDA THOMPSON, Show Host

The Authors Show, www.TheAuthorsShow.com

The Authors Show, Nancy Villella, Production Assistant; TheAuthorsShow.com

The Authors Show, Danielle Hampson, Executive Producer; TheAuthorsShow.com

Thank You All For the Recognition....

Use This Space To Write Down
What You Do To Discover Yourself

_____

_____

_____

_____

_____

_____

_____

_____

_____

_____

Use This Space To Write Down
What You Do To Discover Yourself

Use This Space To Write Down
What You Do To Discover Yourself

_____

_____

_____

_____

_____

_____

_____

_____

_____

_____

Use This Space To Write Down
What You Do To Discover Yourself

_____

_____

_____

_____

_____

_____

_____

_____

_____

Use This Space To Write Down
What You Do To Discover Yourself

_____

_____

_____

_____

_____

_____

_____

_____

_____

_____

Use This Space To Write Down
What You Do To Discover Yourself

_____

_____

_____

_____

_____

_____

_____

_____

_____

Use This Space To Write Down
What You Do To Discover Yourself

_____

_____

_____

_____

_____

_____

_____

_____

_____

Use This Space To Write Down What You Do To Discover Yourself

_____

_____

_____

_____

_____

_____

_____

_____

_____

Use This Space To Write Down
What You Do To Discover Yourself

_____

_____

_____

_____

_____

_____

_____

_____

_____

www.ingramcontent.com/pod-product-compliance
Lightning Source LLC
Chambersburg PA
CBHW071738020426
42331CB00008B/2086